# The Other Side of the Hill

Also by the Capitol Hill Poetry Group
*The Other Side of the Hill, 1979*
*The Other Side of the Hill, 1996*

Capitol Hill Poetry Group

# The Other Side of the Hill
## 1975 – 2025

Patricia Gray
Charise M. Hoge
Mary Ann Larkin
Greg McBride
Nancy Fitz-Hugh Meneely
Jean Nordhaus
Patric Pepper
Noel Salinger
Rosemary Winslow
Anne Harding Woodworth

Pond Road Press
North Truro, Massachusetts

Copyright for poems: © 2025 by the authors.
Copyright for anthology: © 2025 by Pond Road Press.

Cover art: *City Map of Washington D.C., United States,* by SamKal, licensed through Shutterstock.com.

Book design and composition by Mary Ann Larkin and Patric Pepper.

ISBN: 978-1-7336574-4-0

Library of Congress Control Number: 2025944268

Further acknowledgments follow on page 82.

1 2 3 4 5 6 7 8 9 10

Pond Road Press
PO Box 30
North Truro, Massachusetts 02652

patric.pepper@yahoo.com

Available through major online booksellers, Ingram Content Group distribution, and Pond Road Press.

This book is set in Garamond Premier Pro, a font designed for Adobe by Robert Slimbach. This book was printed in the United States of America by Lightning Source LLC, a business unit of Ingram Content Group.

*To*

*Peter Petcoff
who named us*


*and in loving memory of*

*Shirley Cochrane
Ann Knox
Robert Sargent
Elizabeth Sullam
Edwin Zimmerman*

# Contents

Preface

Patricia Gray
- 4 July Full Moon
- 5 Falling
- 6 Crossing the Blue Ridge
- 7 My Uncle's House
- 9 Washington Days

Charise M. Hoge
- 12 Flow
- 13 Wild Goose Chase
- 14 Dead Journalist
- 15 Raw Footage
- 16 For Hire
- 17 Juxtapose
- 18 Nikki Giovanni at Politics and Prose

Mary Ann Larkin
- 20 *IT*
- 22 The Grandmothers
- 23 Those Desert Afternoons
- 24 Angell's Toenails
- 26 A Lock of Patric's Mother's Hair

Greg McBride
- 28 Whistled Alive
- 29 Crossing Over
- 30 In Country: Day One
- 31 Music Lady
- 32 Know Thyself
- 33 Back of the Envelope
- 34 The Buffalo

## Nancy Fitz-Hugh Meneely

- 36 Woman Thinking
- 37 At the Jetty's End
- 38 At Night the House Belongs to Me
- 40 Solstice, December 2024
- 41 How Music Does: Barber's *Adagio for Strings*
- 42 Passing Fair

## Jean Nordhaus

- 44 The Aunts
- 45 Gloves
- 46 The Stammer
- 47 The Innocent
- 48 I Was Always Leaving
- 49 Selling the Porsche
- 50 Old Money

## Patric Pepper

- 52 They're Grackles and Every Time I See Them
- 53 Number 6 Sherman Circle
- 54 Poetry
- 55 Swept
- 57 The Old Home Place Is Inside You

## Noel Salinger

- 60 A Brief Ballet
- 61 String Theory
- 62 The Martin
- 64 Last Words
- 65 On Guard
- 66 Pioneers

## Rosemary Winslow

    68  Going Home
    70  Foxes
    71  Kingdom of Cloth, Three Women, a Naked Boy
    72  Haifa Street, Baghdad
    73  This Quiet Time
    74  Blue Raft

## Anne Harding Woodworth

    76  First Kiss, 1957
    78  Certificates in Safe Deposit
    79  Train Station
    80  Late Summer into Winter
    82  Scripts

## Bios & Acknowledgments

# Preface

Although it's hard to believe, the Capitol Hill Poetry Group has been meeting regularly for 50 years to share and critique our poems. The first tentative sessions took place in 1975 in the kindergarten room of Capitol Hill Presbyterian Church. As confidence grew, we moved from the cramped chairs and low tables in the church basement to the comfort of our living rooms, indulging in food, wine and gossip before the cry, "Let's do poetry." Peter Petcoff, a reference librarian at the Library of Congress and a radiant friend and advisor, named our group, as well as suggesting *The Other Side of the Hill* as a title for our first anthology in 1979. As we wrote in 1996 in the preface to our second anthology, we wanted the name to "identify us as a nonpolitical voice in this most political of cities . . . as a vote for the small, personal human voice in a world where, to use poet Robert Hayden's phrase, 'monsters of abstraction / . . . threaten us.'"

Jean Nordhaus, who along with Shirley Cochrane, founded our group on those kindergarten chairs in 1975, is still a member. Shirley, sadly, has passed on. Throughout the group's fifty years, scores of poets have participated, always in person, but seldom more than six to ten people at a time. During the pandemic years, the workshop made the leap from our homes to the Internet and has continued online, with members living in various states. We meet every two to three weeks now, though, alas, without the wine and cheese.

What has not changed over these many years is our way of working—to quote again from the 1996 anthology: "absolute honesty coupled with respect both for the person and the poem," a commitment neither to praise nor judge but to help each poem, as an act of language, come as close as possible to realizing its ambition.

It has been fifty years. The passing time has brought many books of poems by our members. We meet earlier, but we still laugh and gossip until the familiar cry, "Let's do poetry," puts us to work. Our lives and poems have changed and our world has been made richer over these years, as together we've made space for the imagination. And so, with this third anniversary collection, we invite you back to the other side of the hill, hoping that these poems will give you as much pleasure in the reading as they gave us in the making.

The Capitol Hill Poetry Group

Patricia Gray

## July Full Moon

Born    in a lightning storm
thunder    cracking    sky roof
spirit eye    opening    delivery shaft
branch breaking    falling
street blocked    Buck Moon hiding
out in the reaches    young antlers
pushing through itchy    eager
I was born    under a day-before
Hay Moon    alfalfa cut and baled
stashed from storm    Born
under    a Mead Moon medieval
old pubs peppering    flat beer
to sell it    Born a bumpkin
in The District's    mid-summer
mischief    a sliver of madness in me
switch of lightning    and this
deep clap of    Thunder Moon

# Falling

Just a college boy home on break . . . we knew
each other in third grade,
but it's as if, gazing at you, I'd never seen
a grown man before.
Was it like this when the first humans met—
maybe they showered
at the edge of a waterfall, nipples hardening
as they clung to each other
for warmth against the cold and weather?
Like that, I begin answering
the song in you with the song in me. Like that,
your hands declared
themselves to me, and my hands warmed
the cold in you.
Like that, I brush my lips to your skin, the way
a toddler brushes
her lips to the satin edge of a blanket she loves.
Like that, my arms
and legs and thighs rest on yours. Your arms
and legs and thighs
rest on mine. Our bodies have met their keepers.
Like that,
in pied sunlight, our skin is amber, dappled,
as if holding bits
of ancient animals and plants. We are newborn,
and nothing in us
is new. We are students. We are stardust.

## Crossing the Blue Ridge

Driving over the mountain and into the valley, I hear a rolling sound
like waves coming across fields that once held the fodder
shocks of ancestors' labors, a feeling the soul misses—

I imagine the Iroquois Nation tilling these fields as they moved
their farming in answer to the weather's instructions, and then
back to the deep history when our planet was one big ocean,

and the mountains I love erupted in the Earth's raw turnings,
and the valley pulled away from the foothills, where
the range stretches out in the distance.

The Blue Ridge is like my parents. It blends Dad's muscular
caring with Mom's mind and pillowy curves, as if
she were lying on her side on the horizon.

Patricia, you know you're romanticizing, pretending the landscape
is human. You miss your parents, don't you—now that you're
all grown up and too old to be called an orphan.

## My Uncle's House

I learned from you the elegance of proof,
complex math, and my own inadequacies,
that imagination steals energy from the real world—
and even memory, so tidy and selective,
can be brutal in its sameness from which
the density of touch is vanished,
from which completion is barred,
as it is for the buck leaping at the fence
or the puzzle always being worked on your table.

I have come here, Uncle, for my sanity
that it might stabilize like an object in your room—
like the fox skull you found in a field and baked
till the spiders ran out. If there is any wisdom,
it is in collections such as these,
in the clutter of your nests and shells,
in the gargoyle or geode that waits
to be taken up and turned in the hand
as if some lesson were in it—a clue
to the unfocused excitement it evokes.

Or wisdom might grow from movement,
from the circular sweep of your arm
as you lean over the conch shell puzzle
searching for the shape you must have,
while I rest my cheek on the smooth
leather chair (that sits on the worn rug
slightly off-square) and gaze at the objects
everywhere on ledges: mock-ups, old prints,
open books. It is evening and the curtains

*Gray*

are open. At the window your telescope slants
toward the North Star, as if this house were
a navigable craft and you were to take her home.

## Washington Days

This morning, standing on the sweet spot near the Capitol, where tourists like to stand, I watched workmen heft bollard posts into deep cement pits. On this same spot, you too may stand, deterred by the barriers today being placed. I imagine you, visitor or friend, walking ahead of me in your future-clothes. You will not know the Capitol we have known, nor the area generations before us knew—when the grounds were open and citizens could drive up to the steps, or even earlier, when horses were tied to wrought iron hitching posts later converted to park benches. But if you have already visited, you may know me as the stranger in your family

album, the blurred figure passing through, as you snapped a Washington memory—for I was born here, took first steps holding my parents' hands on Pennsylvania Avenue, the southeast side, away from the residence of power. If you asked directions, I gave them. If requested, I held your camera, opened the quick lens and captured you with the dome, its Statue of Freedom on top—the same statue that was removed to the parking lot for cleaning—a Romanesque figure with a helmet, and not the Native American we had thought.

Just this morning, visitor, I heard, as you will hear, birdsong and twitter, the scattering under feet of squirrels scampering aloft at my approach, the caw-cry of crows in the distance. And today, a cab driver may tell you old stories of neighborhoods in days when doors were left open, cars unlocked, and about Capitol Hill on hottest evenings, when children in nightgowns sometimes slept under low branches on the soft, Capitol grass.

This morning, as usual, dawn runners hurry past, while others, dressed for work, speak brightly into cell phones to no one nearby.

*Gray*

Thriving and busy, the city forms itself around Jersey barriers,
metal check-points—though, still, over there, you may see
the Potomac's mild ripples where swimmers once splashed, men
fished, or others hunted its banks. And just as the tidied-up Potomac
sends its fresh eastward breeze toward the Hill, the neglected
Anacostia will also be cleaned. Have you sculled the Potomac, or
paddle-boated the Tidal Basin? Like you, in April, I have walked
by cherry blossoms sprouting from tree trunks as easily as from
branches, and looked at the pink-tinged blossoms damp after
showers, glistening against rain-blackened bark.

Do I have your confidence? Come here. There is still magic
on this spot and—though the city can be cutthroat in its clubs and
drug dens and neighborhoods overrun and pulled down—on any
street near the Capitol, when the honks and shouts die down and
Congress leaves for the weekend, you can hear the soft scuff
of your shoe soles on the sidewalk, and the city becomes a simple
hometown. Staffers and youngsters come home. A mother pauses
to sit on a bench, lift her blouse and nurse the new infant—its small
hand, only a tenth-size of yours, while indoors, a grandmother pads
in slippers to pick up her newspaper. By now, a line has formed
at the coffee shop, where a Hispanic father continues to hold his own
against the day-to-day forces that, at times, would bring him down.

And, on any given weekend, while the media and cranes doze, when
you pass neighbors on the cobblestone walk, look down at the contours
of tree roots buckling the brick path and remember the poet who walked
here and who tended wounded soldiers on the Mall. Walk farther from
the Hill, past the halfway house where small miracles still occur each
time a life that has died to the root sprouts again past lethal cravings.
Then, you will know that freedom can return. It is possible to step
across rivers of fear and, with feet wet and soiled, find the way, even
as we construct barriers that hide from us the knowledge that once
this city was open and could be again.

Charise M. Hoge

## Flow

backward is wolf
is fur is tracks is dirt
of grasses of lawns
with signs "hate has
no home here"
with sighs of willows
will, oh will we know
neighbors born of
family trees deforested
of stories hoarded
not to end but to bend
into wind whipping
a whip-poor-will
calls a repeated refrain
to cry its name
the ten thousand things
are one and the
same word
forward is flow

## Wild Goose Chase

After the acupuncture, PT, cranio-sacral, EFT,
chiropractic treatment, healing touch,
there's not much difference.

So much for going gluten-free, acquiring
a soundscape machine, dabbing oil of helichrysum.
They're all the same.

But a miracle exists in a figure of speech
thanks to the wild geese
of Mary Oliver:

*"Meanwhile the wild geese, high in the clean blue air,
are heading home again."*
I must head home,

toward the song no one is singing,
into my wrecked hearing, into this unfathomable
soaring of sound. Again.

## Dead Journalist

*for Jamal Khashoggi*

October 2nd.
There's a blank column
staunch as a pillar
on page A27
of *The Washington Post*
reserved for the writer
who would have had
something to say,
who has something to say
by effacement.
The stop of speech
hits like stone, like matter.
But what matters doesn't
… when tangibles tangle
our pleasantries.
The sinews of silence
stand up, stand anyway,
ready to run for their life.

## Raw Footage

We were others' others.
Tooling around boroughs
of the city that never sleeps.
In your car, which cost
a fortune to park.

Unspooling our movie-like
storyline. You called me
pájaro, bird. Named yourself
el brujo, witch. We paused
ready-made futures

in a chronology of life...
starring in a film without
my fiancé, your fiancée.
It plays scene by scene:

in the salsa club /cut/
sushi date /cut/ at the shoreline
riding horses in lieu of weekly
staff meeting /cut/

Until the /cuts/ disappear
for a picnic unscripted which
we don't know how to end.
Sipping wine drinking lips
on the grassy slope
we're falling
into real...

The film snaps.
Its fluttering sound echoes
your huarache clogs
clapping sidewalks, on and on.
A few loose blonde wisps
cling to your passenger seat
when I leave.

## For Hire

No matter how you angle it,
an angel stands by...
beyond the flourish framed in canvas,
stained glass, bronze cast, perched at the pietà.
Winged or not, steadfast as a tour guide,
muted. You may dispute me.
Mais, les anges. Les anges.

In the fog of the roadway, I lose
my bearings. Yasmine, beside me,
wastes no time to confide, "you know,
a lot of unemployed angels are out there."
Oh, her clarity. No trumpet resounds
when my outlook steadies.
Mais, les anges. Les anges.

## Juxtapose

When the body reclines
to raise a leg like a quill
dipped in the hip's
inkwell,
to circle the miracle
of ball-and-socket
(the quill beholden
to the inkwell,
the leg beholden
to the acetabulum)
looping cursive

writing on the ceiling
(hieroglyphical)
that decodes
as eyes close,
tickling the inner ear
at rest in the eider-
down of dreams (lucid),

dreams where the dearly
departed
sometimes dwell—
just suppose Dorothy
Parker (likely a stand-in
for the Dorothy who
carried me into being)
inscribes in the ether:
all your relief
   will be
sun and rain.

## Nikki Giovanni at Politics and Prose

We must have been numb
while she was hip she was
here: "I am a beautiful woman."

She paused all of a sudden,
choppers overriding her buzz.
We... must have been numb.

DCers, what had we become,
she teased. We had not budged.
Where am I... "a beautiful woman"?

Airlift, the fall of Saigon?
Unfazed, blasé our bias
has been. Must we numb...?

Perched on her chair lissome
as a gazelle, quick her prowess.
Here I am, a beautiful woman.

How the reading of the room
and her poetry coalesced.
We have been, mostly, numb.
Hear: "I am a beautiful woman."


Note: "I am a beautiful woman" is a line from
"Ego-Tripping (there may be a reason why)."

Mary Ann Larkin

## IT

Sister Clementine felt *it*
though I never did
until I read Levine's poem
about the boys, ferocious
and happy, playing with the milkweed
on their way to that hated school.
*It* is why Sister put us in rows
from the smartest to the dumbest.
I never thought about that either
except for feeling a little sorry
for poor Frankie Scaliano
with his Baby Jesus eyes
big and dark and puzzled.
Did he know, I wonder now,
why he was in the last seat
in the last row?
Did anyone know?
Or was *it* just a dream we dreamed,
what the Buddhists call a delusion,
something, maybe nothing,
like a string of camels in the desert,
seen from far away
and never wondered about.
Because we did not wonder
why Sister Clementine
laid us out like times tables.
But the poem about the boys
and the milkweed
made me get Sister Clementine
and all of us in our boxy desks
with lids we were forbidden to open,

holding our wax paper sandwiches,
and the notes we passed
about who liked who.
I saw *it* hulking
above us, though, of course,
I didn't see *it*. No one did.
But *it* was there, instructing
Sister Clementine about her seating charts,
the ones she made like a good girl
after evening prayers. And I saw
how *it* hovered over the world,
the city, our parents' houses
and how even they bowed to it
and made obeisance and mumbled yes
and stuffed us into leggings and mittens
and unseeing, sent us on our way,
past the milkweed,
to Sister Clementine.

## The Grandmothers

The grandmothers stand
silent as mountains,
make caves of their bodies
where the children curl like bats
gibbering for their mothers.

The grandmothers pay no heed,
sorrow just a rain that falls.
They stand past sadness, outside
indifference and justice, more solid
than what we call love.

## Those Desert Afternoons

The heat exhaling
a breath just short of burning,
as though across the dusty porch
some somnolent beast padded,
myself half-awake on the plump pillows
of that sheet-draped couch.
The baby beside me,
bat-mouthed, bird-boned.
The sun high, almost hidden.
A copper haze. And the stillness.
Only shadows moved.

Evenings, we breathed deeply again.
I showered, sweat-damp
as though from love. The baby
tottered around. The sun
arced away. Coolness coming
as though the rumored beast
had at last inhaled us
into spongy lungs and slept.

I can't tell you how it was,
but I gave myself
to those desert afternoons
the same way the baby,
knowing nothing of denial,
fell upon the breast—
with just that amount of birthright
and greed.

## Angell's Toenails

Dianne Cargill's moment came
when Angell, dying, could no longer
paint her toenails luster peach.
Only Dianne noticed the flaking opalescence
where once all had been as satin-smooth
as the color of a sunrise in a fairy tale book.
Angell loved fairy tales and knowing
about Bailey's Beads, how they circled the throat
of the moon every 99 years,
and van Loon's story about eternity.
Dianne knew about jobs and money
and schedules. She went to meetings
and had a phone, into which she entered
Angell's toenails.

And so it was, Saturday at nine:
Angell in her pale-green Japanese kimono
with herons curving round her arms,
now as thin as the birds' necks.
Dianne propped her up
on the wicker chair's paisley pillows,
settled herself on Aunt Ginny's oriental
and poured oil of lavender,
to soften the hard Cleveland water,
into the blue spatter ware bowl.
Taking Angell's dwindling feet in her hands,
Dianne stroked the oil
even between Angell's toes,
reawakening her tired blood.

And Angell watched and understood
and gave her feet into Dianne's hands
and spoke of the color peach
and foxes' feet, their song,
and how lavender heals,
and said that when a bird
wears away a mountain
by sharpening his beak
once every thousand years,
one day of eternity passes,
and told Dianne that the touch of flesh
is kin to God.

Dianne Cargill, curls coiled tight
above the steaming water, listened
as she gravely restored to Angell's toes
the mystery of luster peach,
and took from Angell
something Dianne needed
but could not name.
And somewhere between the lavender
and Angell's paper-thin flesh,
between the talk of foxes and eternity,
something came undone in Dianne Cargill,
so that, before continuing on Saturday's rounds,
she sat in her car and wept.

## A Lock of Patric's Mother's Hair

Dark with a little silver,
curved like a crescent moon
in a box just a bit larger
than the lock itself.
It's 2015 now. The lock, 30 years old.
Patric has kept it all these years,
even before I knew him.
Now he will part with it.
When I try to fathom how
he made this decision,
I see a kind of flow chart
of small angles and dotted lines
pointing to other paths,
all of them leading
to the marsh behind our cottage,
where the lock will go—sometime soon.
Patric wants a redwing to make a nest of it.
We are waiting for a good day,
the two of us, an unhurried day.
Misty would be all right
or sunny and dry with a breeze.
I'd like to read a poem
beside the marsh—a poem about hair
and grief, with a little hope in it.
But, somehow, I keep picturing
the way oxen, patient and silent
stand by a gate.

Greg McBride

## Whistled Alive

Late fall, the world again closing in
upon itself. Nights extend, days stall,
and the chill takes hold of Pennsylvania.
We hibernate under artificial light
in the practice room where wrestling coaches
bark enduring truths then whistle us alive
in this rite reserved for the quick, the strong,
the sinewy light doggedly wary.
This must be some kind of love, this shutting out,
shutting in, this drain of self into self,
more weight to shoulder through our hunger.
We shuffle and tender sugarfeet.
He's a mirror-me: I claw, he claws, heads butt,
hands seize sweat-slick muscle. I collar him,
rough a forearm hard to his clavicle,
stutter-step. Balance, balance is all.
I am stronger, faster. So say tight grips,
the hurried brawl. I flash to a leg;
he drops to splay his weight over me,
the way soggy nautical rope might feel—
knotty, tentacular, doughy. He grabs
my head, wheels on the axis he makes of me.
His strength meets mine, I parry his every move
(each the other reified). The mild sorrow
of blood rises warm in my mouth.
He's on his back! I power down, but he rears
unstoppably from the mat. Sudden loss,
sudden win. We practice both, again, again.
No winner here, it's him, myself, I pin.

# Crossing Over

*above the Pacific, January 1969*

Rows ahead, rows behind, soldiers hunch
into themselves in the ghostly quiet
of this chartered, carpeted 707,
jungle fatigues bloused at boot tops.
Ventilation panels flank our ankles
for Southeast Asian heat to come.
We are dog-tagged numbers dangling
on beaded chains, but the Army covers
all bets: blood type, religion, metallic name.
I'm a child beside an infantry captain
whose silence sprawls over the armrest
into my space. He fumbles a passel
of photos, shuffles a wife, blond kids.
He's a mountain, sloped, bucolic, stoic.
Our porthole's a tondo of black sky, stars.
I conjure my mother, father, sister,
a paddy in which to hide. The stewardess
attends us tenderly, and as she leans in
to ask what I'd like, her hair, so clean,
falls toward her lips, and one fine strand
shines free. She slips away through jet-whine,
enfleshing what feels like abandonment.

## In-Country: Day One

Duffel bag stuffed in the back, he bounced down
Cong Ly on the suicide seat. The sergeant crowed
they'd stolen the mud-scarred jeep the night
before on a Cholon whorehouse street.
His starched jungle fatigues and boots were a joke
in a city of thousands, .45 hard
on his hip. Dressed in yellow, Saigon hummed
like a factory. Fuel-stench hung like a scrim.
The sun seared down on angels in *ao dais,*
silk panels in a red soft as wet blood,
in the green of his mother's eyes.
They skimmed the simmering sidewalks,
at ease in their beauty under the palm-leaf
shade of conical *nons,* the calm rise
of dry heat, skirts wafting in spiraled mists
of *nuoc mam,* the smog of fried steam rolls.
That night, he sauntered down Tu Do Street.
The bar girls called and the cyclos spat
their two-cycled rasp. Distant iron bombs dropped
from B-52s burst out of the dark,
laying a blanket of moans over him
and the street and the girls too young in the night.
He glanced at the stars and felt himself
holding onto his gun with both hands.

# Music Lady

My wife is in the kitchen making
kitchen sounds, odd arhythmic tunes
she's always played: the skillet slide
across a grate, the counter thump,
the scrape along a carrot length,
tunes that somehow call to mind
her birthing cry, her calves and inner thighs
in nylon, scuffing one another,
back when she could walk in heels.
In those days, the music drew us in,
slow-dancing close at night,
lights dimmed in the family room,
the kids asleep, the Divine
Sarah Vaughan on the stereo,
or Miss Peggy Lee vamping a saxophone.
Because we can no longer dance,
the music only now remains.
She speaks of something into
an empty room, her voice-tones round
and shushed.          Her good leg drags the bad
across the kitchen's hardwood floor the way
a jazz brush slurs a snare drum's skin.

## Know Thyself

I'm an old man now, getting to know myself,
my marbles still neatly arranged, like my taws
and cat's eyes in Quaker Oats boxes Mother
saved for me. But this morning, scratching an itch,
I noticed that my wrist is tiny, tiny telling lies.
So I checked a leg—my mighty quadriceps,
which have powered my life of runs and matches,
so many steps—and was appalled. Now,
there have been hints of a certain smallness
since starting out at six pounds, but this
—what can only be called a boy-sized leg
flexing in a failing crop of white leg hair—
gave me a start. I'm ridiculous it seems.
Do others know? I think of fun with my wife
in bed when I'd whisper, "Go ahead,
cop a feel of my *massive thigh*" (always
italicized), and she'd ooh and ahh
while stroking my strong, bowed legs, my grandpa legs.
She was in on the joke, I only sort of. I've run
for miles, lifted weights, done squats, climbed
up and down stairs, but it seems I've been gilding
a miniature lily. It seems this self I've carried
through time and place has been poorly housed
all along. My advice to young people:
As you make your way through life, check now
and then to be sure you know who you are.
You may be smaller than you thought.

## Back of the Envelope

You're still drowsing upstairs, crumpled
    under the comforter. I'm in the kitchen,
wrapped in my robe at breakfast, peering
    through swoops of frost at sun-bathed snow outside:
the veiled lawn and stubble, lamp post, roll and roll
    beyond the pond, the sheen a mile to the pines.
I'm doodling on a security envelope,
    a #10—so handy for shopping lists,
for reckoning mortgage amortizations,
    for juggling our shrunken life expectancy
with income, savings, expenditures,
    for indulging arithmetic fantasy:
that our last dollar might be spent on our last day.
    This time, though, I'm thinking about last night:
how in our heat we smoldered into sleep
    before we could re-sense or re-dress ourselves,
how we melded to embrace our warmth,
    the way a cabin stoked for night turns in
upon itself, snow-draped in winter woods,
    how we woke in the quiet of first-light,
eyes on eyes, lips pouting with last night's love.
    Hmm. 31.5 times 365,
plus eight leap days, and days magnified
    by Saratoga, San Francisco, Princeton,
Portland, all of it compounded over years.
    I hope you'll come downstairs soon. I've made
coffee and a fire. I've found some old photos
    that show us in our strength.
I'll put on the mackinaw and tuque,
    shovel to the shed to get the sled, and soap
its runners well. But first, let's watch the logs
    rearrange themselves in their diminishment,
how the embers crackle stars until the very end.

## The Buffalo

He must have known years of snow,
flakes slanting as if thrown like stones
into his ageless eyes, onto his brow,
his matted beard. This time, perhaps
he'd got his hopes up, perhaps he'd been misled,
the way the crocus and the daffodil
miscalculate an early spring.

The wind-blown snow picks up, his hooves dig in,
and the cold's a creeping vise upon his bones.
He hunches on a rise to watch the vast
and quiet grassland and knows he's ranged
too far from granite clefts or Dakota
cottonwoods. He's patient as his nickeled
image lying worn on a long loblolly bar.

Sixty million gone:  their tongues to the hungry
and unspeakable; their scrotums laced
as pouches holding dice carved from their bones;
hides for saddles, stirrups, lariats;
beards for mittens. Blood for paint.

Nancy Fitz-Hugh Meneely

## Woman Thinking

I am reading a book about a painting
and as I look up to think I see
that my window frames
a perfect rendering of a wood
that is infinite within
and then I feel I make a picture
of a woman thinking wistfully
and understand there is no way
to tell what lies behind the eyes of
all those famous painted women
because I myself am trying to decide
if an afternoon snack deserves dessert.

## At the Jetty's End

I try to find a poem
to hold the surge of ocean
concentrated here, the instant
when combers press
from the south and west,
the ocean folding itself
into clefts no word could swim.
I want to carry the storm
back home in a sonnet, say,
but there are no lines
that wouldn't succumb
to the suck of the sea
already swallowing
the clouds, the air, itself.

## At Night the House Belongs to Me

*Gettysburg, 1983*

The quiet isn't quite complete.
Our old house sighs
beneath the weight of dark and cold.
A single car's a whisper
in the village street and I can hear
the hum of dishes washing,
radiators singing protest
as the heat comes on,
muted notice that the night
though full of peace is not asleep.

The hall light glows and shadow
frames the wicker rocking chair
where I will nurse my child
before the night is through.
She's snoring softly, one arm flung
between the bars of her crib
as if she'd attempted a getaway
before the rest of her
surrendered to the hour.

In their third floor aerie
my husband's sons are dreaming,
perhaps of the days before
their mother let them go.
Morning often finds the older
bleeding bitterness, the younger
longing fruitlessly.

*Meneely*

But this night seems to offer
tendering, our motley family
joined in rest.

My husband drowses
in our bed, arms and legs
stretched either way
so half of him can warm
the place where I will lie.
He'll turn himself away
when I slip underneath
the sheet we share
and I will fit my back
into the curve of his,
as safe as ever I have felt.

## Solstice, December 2024

Earlier tonight, a gibbous moon
rose from the dark behind the shoulder
of a hill, skimmed the river sliding
toward the Sound and glazed
the frozen grasses on its banks.
Partway full, she lit a thinning film of cloud.

Now halfway high, she pours her luster
through the leafless trees to wash
against a house across the street,
her silver light uniting with the gold
and homely of a family's corner room.
I want to feel myself inside the scene,
a part of both the solitude of moonlight
and the warmth of someone reading by a lamp.
But the tableau doesn't hold; the moon
moves on too soon to join the deep cold height
and company of stars.

These years it seems to me that time
has gone awry. Although it dawdles
between lunch and dinnertime,
the weeks careen, the moments I would wish
to hold to heart retreat to past.

I can't afford this race of days.
I haven't said the all I meant.
The year expires
before I've loved enough.

# How Music Does: Barber's *Adagio for Strings*

> *We wish the ear had not a heart*
> *so dangerously near.*
> Emily Dickinson

First chair, she tucks her instrument beneath her chin,
rests it gentle on her arm. The maestro lifts his hands
and in the pause before he lets them fall,
he asks her with his eyes. She lowers hers
and answers, bow both soft and sure across the strings.
The strings begin to weep. Something close to anguish
concentrates her face.
She's making sorrow out of sound.

Longing fugitive in us begins to ache again
as deeper strings come in. We feel the music
low inside ourselves, the place
where we have kept the inexpressible.
It troubles silence there.

The strings insist on sadness that is all of ours
but as the long and final note releases me,
I find myself in sorrow that is singular.
Self-centered in this nameless grief,
I carry it away alone, those around me
solitary, too.

## Passing Fair

When I die, misfortune now foreseeable,
I'd rather not that it be said of me
that I have passed. I don't exactly misbelieve
that others travel on to endless golden futures
in a sunblown landscape ceaselessly in bloom
where night falls only so the slow exhale
of tree and flower can rectify the air.

But when I die, all that I am then will park
in time. I'll occupy until time's end
my childhood room where light
slipped through the louvered shades
to fall in slivers on my hands
until the moon moved on
and I was left in darkness, sweet enclosure
inside boundlessness.

I want my child to picture me
that way, in perfect comfort,
snugged as deep as I can go
beneath the covers of a night
that is by some design just cold enough.

Jean Nordhaus

## The Aunts

When they came
breathing jasmine and raspberry,
tinkling the charms on their bracelets,
money and sweets
in the folds of their skirts,
heads haloed in lamps,
voices high and sweet as rosewater,
shedding powder and perfumed fur,
the wild smells gone,

When bathed and barefoot
I curled in their caverns of fur
drowning in sweet,
foxes bit themselves
into chains around their shoulders,
jade eyes tracing the circle of years:
emphysema, insomnia, bad faith,
powdered faces puckered, eyes
hot, perjured.

Turning into tigers
yellow as tallow
they chased each other
around the tree, tooth to tail
running faster, faster
blur of heat and wind until they—
butter, oh, butter would, butter would
melt in the sweet, sweet caverns
of their mouths.

# Gloves

When all the birds roost
suddenly
the bare tree
bursts into leaf.

Plumb, tapered, brown, true
a flock of
weathervanes
nosing into

the wind, they hang to
the branches
like gloves, then
leave suddenly

leaving the branches,
the branches
full of in-
visible hands.

## The Stammer

We are two-minded, my tongue and I.
It is always like this: I mean
to say *That house is tall.*
or *God is one.* But the tongue
has another opinion. It wants

to be heard. We are like Mishnah,
two sparrows disputing
a morsel of law. I grapple
with my tongue as Jacob
wrestled with the angel

for a word. From this clash
of intentions I've learned
to hold back, to listen:
the voice at my shoulder when I
try to speak, saying

*Wait.* The tongue
is a caged beast, an animal
wild to escape. Compel it
and it will elude you. Released,
it will yield to your lightest

desire. Soft, and the sounds that need
to speak themselves will flow.
Be gentle and the words
will come like deer
to water or a woman to love.

## The Innocent

Alone and together, we stand on the platform,
a mob of strangers awaiting a train. There may be
among us a wife-beater; surely, a thief. That man
in the blue dolphin tie; that frazzled woman,
gathering in her scattered girls; each of us caught
in the swill of our being; none of us blameless,
not one of us pure. Greedy, covetous,
selfish, vain, we have trafficked in lies; we
have practiced small cruelties. Even the baby,
asleep in a sling on his mother's breast,
has been willful, has shaken with rage.

Yet if fate arrives as a wind, in a bullet,
a bomb, at the moment of shock, in the silent
heart of conflagration, we will all
be transformed into innocents, cleansed
in the fires of violence, punished not for any sins
committed—but for standing where we stand,
together in the soft, the vulnerable flesh.

## I Was Always Leaving

I was always leaving, I was
about to get up and go, I was
on my way, not sure where.
Somewhere else. Not here.
Nothing here was good enough.

It would be better there, where I
was going. Not sure how or why.
The dome I cowered under
would be raised and I would be released
into my true life. I would meet there

the ones I was destined to meet.
They would make an opening for me
among the flutes and boulders
and I would be taken up. That this
might be a form of death

did not occur to me. I only know
that something held me back—
a doubt, a debt, a face I could not
leave behind. When the door
fell open I did not go through.

## Selling the Porsche

For over a year it lay in the garage
bedded beside my homely Subaru

long, lean, muscular, beautiful,
bought in the joy of remission

six summers ago, in an access of hope.
It was there when I drove out each morning,

the battery long dead, though once it roared,
and there at night when I slid in beside it,

docking snugly in my narrow slip.
I was tough, sorting, tossing, warding off,

but when the driver came
with his dinosaur tow-truck, hauled

the body up the ramp and drove away
I went inside and had to sit, and a shrill trail

of unfamiliar whoops rose from my throat
rose from that primeval cave where all the winds

contend—aboriginal death wails,
ululations of abandoned brides.

Who is this woman, I wondered?
Who are all these women howling through me?

## Old Money

I don't mean "aristocracy" or "class"
just these old coins saved
in a rusted tin among paper clips,
staples, rubber bands, dust.

The shaven countenance
of childhood's President
has grown a fuzzy beard of lint.
The beauty on the Liberty dime

(Wallace Stevens' quiet wife)
has lost her luster. And the nickel—
on the nickel, Thomas Jefferson
has almost rubbed away.

What to do with these icons
of analog days? Old money.
It has slept a long time
in the dark losing value.

Shall I shut the lid and let it sleep
another thirty years? So much
is lost or seems to be ebbing away.
America. *In God We Trust.*

So pluck it out, brush it off,
and let it mingle with the new.
Let it know again the touch
of hands, the thrill and lust

of commerce. Spend it. Spend it.

Patric Pepper

## They're Grackles and Every Time I See Them

I scrawl my admiration in my all-weather birder book.
I don't really have an all-weather birder book; I have
just the one in my mind, where I'm free to scratch.
                                      The grackles cluck
to have their say, and I like that. Sometimes they swell
and hop and spread dark wings and perch on my shoulder
                              and have a look
          in my birder book.

Which is to say they examine my self-assured scratch
with their ESP black eyes that chill the spine
with their golden-zero fat-chance good-luck pupils—and
      then they double-cluck and flap and bolt pell-mell.
                          In my birder book

I make up little verses (not really) that point in all uncertain
terms to how crooked they're not, and how they,
                              the grackles,
invented the spoon, the hallmark of genius tails that steer
them as they buck and bolt away from *Homo sapiens* insults
like: "Trash birds!" and "Not worthy of poetry!" and "Filthy!"
    These misapprehensions I forgive, and then scribble
                        in my birder book.

## Number 6 Sherman Circle

In this    my 70th year    like a time traveler    from a grade
B movie    I wander back    to a few months before
they married    in 1943    wander to    her very own room
in a house full    of young women    working women all
at number 6 Sherman Circle NW    I watch    the two of them
mount    the steps    to her front door    I watch
her    rifle her purse for the key    I see them    feverishly
in love    oh find the key    this Tuesday afternoon
everyone at work    they at the most important work    of all
and when she finds the key    she turns    to him    and they
embrace    soon to be    true lovers    the two of them
smoldering like the bodies    of Bergman & Bogart    as if
they are one    which they are    watch her    pull the door &
lock it shut    watch them mount    the last staircase
into their    very own room    and    she locks the ultimate door
their love tingling    having blossomed into    lust    I watch
them undo    each other    the 40s dress    blue & white
modest shoulder pads    left on the seat    of a straight-back chair
with his Army greens thrown    on the back of the chair    in this
my 70th year    her stockings    of ever-straight seams    draped
over his jacket    his spit & polish shoes    dropped    his tie
tossed    and soon at last    they embrace    naked as naked gets
I watch them    fall    into the narrow bed    pull    each other
into the wide    forgiving fiery demanding twin bed    to join
forever    now    in lust    which is their love    this first
afternoon    of their proper life    tongue to tongue    red nails
running through his hair    his hands inching down    her back
they cleave    he in her    she enveloping him    before her
housemates return    on the bus from downtown    as American
bombers    practice    in the sky    in this my 70th year

# Poetry

These evenings ambling through the metropolis, through the West End on to Georgetown, these nights you feel as if you've cut a button from your coat and swallowed it, intent, the way a turnstile eats a token, these nights you stroll, dreaming you don't dream, attentive, fresh, across the cobblestones, angling toward some outstretched river through air as warm and smooth as blood, the traffic like a miracle at your back, as you limp on the walk with the pain of the old injury, as five young girls from France line up like sparrows along the hotel fence to say small sentences, which you understand, not knowing French, five girls—fourteen?—all of them smoking the same brand from the same pack,

as a gorgeous man completely fills a black tee with his black body, nipples at attention, pecs and abs designed to raise up Michelangelo, as the man churns with a gorgeous fair-haired woman who climbs on giant heels and California legs, pumping her short skirt with such brave, machine-like harmonies that free beneath the blouse her breasts bounce with delight in time and space, as in the vacant doorways homeless sit, saddened by all that is and isn't in their cups, free imprisoned people asking for mercy,

as traffic lights change, and the crowds walk, and the automobiles lurch and go, you find that you are the city's voice, a pencil scratch on paper, now, when the city is whole and prime, in this its only moment—you find tonight as you barely breathe that death is quite the same as life.

If the French girls could hear your thoughts would they not laugh?—*au contraire!* And the splendid man would fall in love, as would the splendid woman, and small of heart as you've been, the homeless men might take you in, like an exotic potted plant they'd chanced upon downtown, trundled in a grocery cart to beneath the bridge of the wide river where the ferry used to start, where now is only rubble, where now you would blazon the bare Earth about their sleeping bags, a flower blooming in this their era—all of them, all of us, specimens of paradise.

## Swept

It finally seemed right this morning,
after all the puffed-up love poems I'd written her,
after all the years that swept on by like sand storms,
to sweep the kitchen floor
while I waited for the tea water to boil.

Thus it happened that the significant women
I have known, save for one,
significant to me as friends, mothers and others,
few as they have been, a dozen or so,
those ghostly ones and those among us upright still,
stood in the hall, so to speak,
just beyond the kitchen doorway,
watching and kibitzing.

They said to each other, "Look at him."
"Yes! Sweeping the kitchen floor like a young monk!"
At this they chuckled without restraint.
One said, "Amazing." Another responded,
"Yes, amazing what a little zazen will do for a man."

They were all there, except of course
the most significant other ever.

She just a moment ago yawned in the white loft,
then fluttered her voice in unconscious imitation
of the robins and finches beyond the cottage windows.
Soon she descended the steps one at a time,
walked right through my audience,
peeled a banana while looking out the kitchen window,

*Pepper*

counted the tulips in the lily
garden, and said,
"We have 51 tulips this year.
I just counted them."

And just now I sip my tea
and notice in my still proud,
though anonymous, heart
how she doesn't notice the sand
not sticking to her feet.

## The Old Home Place Is Inside You

> *Forecasts indicate that the last snow will fall in 2025.*
> —Comment at the end of the film
> *Never Gonna Snow Again*

You wish to stand in winter's pewter light
At four o'clock with other old men
You had known all your life, had loved all your life,
      to stand by the hay barn
Next to Mr. Walbert's hay wagon, dredge up
      hogwash to laugh about,
*Remember that time? . . . You remember!* Then ask,
      *Is Preston still alive? . . . Drinking?*
Each of you furtively waiting for the snow to begin
      the blessing that it is.
You wish you had always bathed in the creek,
      spring into winter,
The creek that ran through Patton Hollow,
      and that you still did bathe in that creek.
You wish that your house was no house at all
But a tumbledown affair of clapboard
      and mud-stuffed chinks,
The grayed-out boards lapping down the sides,
Newspaper pasted to the inside walls to keep
      out the dispiriting wind,
You wish you had never bought a car,
      had never ridden in a car,
      had never heard of a car.
You wish you had walked everywhere,
      everywhere
No matter how far you had to walk to get to
      EVERYWHERE,

*Pepper*

              which is HERE.
You wish like a broken vow;
        you wish for poverty,
So that time itself might've discontinued travel
        before this graceless culmination took hold.
You wish for that even as you'd reach your own demise
        sooner than later—
You wish to look time in the face and say, Take me home!—
        Who the hell ARE *you?*
You don't wish for money, sex, power, dark chocolate,
        Kenyan tea, good whiskey, happy sunshine
        painting the waking world, nor to NOT die—
You wish for repentance for these foregoing lies—
        and you wish for love
        and forgiveness
        and snow.
You wish to be put to harness, a quiet willing mule
        who'd pull with all the other mules
The sputtering Earth back to its modest but certain orbit
        around its godlike Sun.

Noel Salinger

## A Brief Ballet

Above the barn's horizon
a flight of swallows rises
to a thinning lapis sky.

They wheel and spin,
an obsidian blade,
then stall and quake.

I'm lost in this brief ballet,
birds leaping in unison
as if each knows its steps.

Or each is merely a cell, a sinew
of a momentary wing
soaring to the pale light.

They rise once more, bank
and dissolve behind the barn
into the failing rose of day

as do we all.

## String Theory

Barely dawn, I tiptoe downstairs
avoiding the squeaks.
Not even the grandkids are up.

On the patio, in the still gray cool,
Glück's *The Wild Iris* lies unopened on my lap.
Perhaps one of her matins is in order.

Instead, I watch a jay explore the brush,
then fly to a branch and cry out
a warning of rain.

An unseen thread binds me to the jay,
to the sleeping kids, my wife; dreaming,
the dog snoring upstairs.

The naked air resting
among the oaks
fills my misting breath.

The jay has flown
taking something of me away
but the *Iris* remains on my lap.

I turn to her matins
and am bound to the words
if not the poet's lone sorrow.

## The Martin

My father's Martin is finally home.
Two months of intensive care,
cracked bridge, bent fingerboard, rusted strings.

It was radical surgery. Severed neck,
dismembered body, graft of glue,
transplants of rosewood and faux ebony.

He'd like it, I think,
his 1952 D18 from San Francisco
body restored, but not his old songs

long unplayed,
the simple strums that filled us
with wonder as children

seeing Irene in my dream,
Aunt Rhody's old gray goose,
the black, black hair of his true love.

And now, each day closer to the age he died,
I hold it on my knee and strain
to wrap my knotted fingers around its neck,

to recall the tunes of my rebellions,
when I spun the latest LPs, resetting the needle
over and over to learn tunes of the day

*Salinger*

where the flowers have all gone
is the eve of destruction,
but don't think twice.

This day my fingers ache, my voice clots.
I lay the Martin across its old gray case and it whispers
"I will always belong to him."

## Last Words

*Winston Churchill died January 24, 1965*

At that fated day and hour,
Churchill stirred from his coma,
opened his eyes and said, "I am bored with it all,"
then transitioned, as it is nowadays called.

Bored? My God!
Surely, I can think of something better.

True, I have known no kings or queens,
stiffened no national upper lip,
launched no flotilla to save the boys
or sailed with two pals in big coats to divvy up Europe.

These days I'm left in the dust of this world of deal.
I know no emoji or avatar.
No meme or troll am I.
Such as it is, my intelligence is real.

When my hour arrives
let me open my eyes and offer hope.
"Don't fret, the creek will always run,
the egret will, one day, return."

And may what's next
be a dignity
up with which
I will gladly put.

## On Guard

Sentinel of the last open acres
of farmland in these parts,
a towering tupelo guarded against
invading sheetrock and vinyl siding.

For decades its tree houses
delighted farm kids,
year after year it fledged
bluebirds, cardinals, yellow finches.

Haloed by a leafy summer crown,
growing a snowy beard in the cold,
like a tutelary deity it stood
to keep the land free

until undone by a wee beetle,
rains that rotted roots,
winds that swept away its coif
and felled one arm after another.

A skeleton now in a wiry coat of vines,
farmers gone, the land tangled in court,
its last branch still points to the ground—
*don't you dare.*

## Pioneers

Steel sky, winter wanes.
Wild onions pioneer the forest floor
pungent with life.
The low creek, patient, waits for rain.

A stand of beech, pregnant
with buds, one cluttered
with apostrophes of crows
as if to say, it's ours.

I walk this path often.
Once more I pause at the high point
to survey the creek below,
silver vein through ribs of sycamore.

I close my eyes to survey my self.
Unlike the onion spikes,
the watching crows,
it is not there.

Only a tangle of tales I tell myself,
some of them true.

Rosemary Winslow

## Going Home

There is no going home
as usual
the vehicle stalls
in reverse gear
in mud tracks

as essential as
the flat fields, the blades
of shadowed pines over the drive,
the sun bleeding
from the west.

On the rise the house,
painted clapboard the color of cream,
is rented now like bodies
of water and minerals made
living by some miracle

which is to say some process
we don't understand.
Someday we'll have a
different owner,
a different lover,

like pines trees and whirling wind
that primitive communion
like a new testament
of each generation.
All going home is never going back—

*Winslow*

there may be ruin, and mud tracks
deep to make wheels spin. The only way
is slogging on,
or else walking
on water.

Or yet it may be dry
sand flying in your nostrils
but you must breathe, must go, must go
on, which is to say, go on making
required visits, like stations

of a cross. It is a way
of finding what we'd lost
or never had, of learning we are only
renters, and making new covenants,
of going where we belong.

# Foxes

They are alive somewhere
in the block of blackness that is trees,
the two foxes whose gold eyes
locked and gleamed as our headlights pried
nothing out of them, who waved off
through a door they made in the grasses.

We had stopped to look at the stars.
No cloud, no moon, and the world's
electric dimming three hundred miles away.
We were looking up, your breath stirred
tendrils on my neck, your wet mouth
was atop my head, I was a grass

waving. It was our first night, you
were a stranger. Fragments
of constellations whirled, wildness
cabled down through the woods, you went
into me, I went into you, some kind of light
wheeled as we stood, we were a grass

entered. Black heaven was alive,
had reached us across immeasurable spaces.
And was there as we drove back,
and was waiting all through the days
I did not know how to love you.
You waited, and we grew like grasses.

## Kingdom of Cloth, Three Women, a Naked Boy

Beautiful the light washing him
as he lies, rich-dark as loam
on the rough cloth, as if the strong
sun of Africa exalts this one
who sleeps with a smile of heaven.

Three women hold his head,
his arms. They are covered in
rough cloth, the same rough cloth
spread under him. It is the color
of bleached wheat, of uncut canvas.

What are they doing? Who are they?
Three windows in their burkas
reveal their eyes, creased—with age?
Some right of passage? A sign?—
The dead are were sewn into shrouds...

No, I say, no—this boy almost a man,
perfect of face, limb, the two ladders
of ribs—ineffable peace—ten fingers,
ten toes. Two sperm pockets, limp penis...

The first time I held my own child,
I counted, relieved, all the perfections.
A world to ourselves. What do they see?
His loveliness? their love? famine's
exactions?... the cloth about to close...

*After a photograph by James Nachtwey*
*Somalia, 1993*

## Haifa Street, Baghdad

Far down the stuccoed tunnel they come,
camouflage, rifles, helmets, from the blue
smudge end that is the vanishing point
that is sky, freedom, flight. They stride

in line, deliberate, serious like the eight
boys huddled around a bicycle strung
with yellow and red pennants, with blue-
threaded wheels, who've stopped playing

who are watching the men. They squint
in the loud sun, the sun narrows their eyes—
what will they become? You've a lifetime—
too late, their eyes are captured, desire shot

down to their marrow, streaked with play,
with the good dirt of Haifa like the driveway
my brothers stood in one day, sun—
squinting, toy rifles straight on their shoulders,

straight backs, straight line, three strong
boys captured at play, kept in the family
album, saved, saved before they knew
where they were going.

*After a news photograph*
*May 2005*

## This Quiet Time

Today the house is quiet, no rush hour churning through the street
No birds in the maples and dogwoods, not one helicopter, not one star
No sun dissipates the stone sky
A lone man in a spring jacket strains on a leash behind
    a Golden Retriever
A lone one—everyone is inside or at the grocery, hospital, pharmacy,
    police, or fire
Yesterday construction workers rode the cranes and elevators,
    buildings going up on Sixth and K
Today no one . . . is all the world learning to slow down?
The Japanese magnolia's blossoms turn brown and flop on the walk
In New York Justin and Sarah's wedding is "postponed to July"
For everything there is a season
Wait   Wait in your own house   Wait
The glove that fits the hand stays in the closet, the hat on the shelf
I count every hair in my comb    Someone deducts it from my total
Every breath out of my mouth is numbered
Every sparrow that falls is seen by something unseen
The media says Everyone matters    Some say Don't believe it
Out in the street maples burst with tiny leaves, up close they look
    like miniature hands
Linden blossoms and leaves silently bide their time
I notice the white on the window frames outside is whiter . . .
    I put down my pen
Oh, the sun must be coming . . . there's a shine now on
    Deborah's bay window
Now it's gone as a rumble of a truck sweeps through the canyon of air

## Blue Raft

The phoebes' asthmatic rasp, 4 on the radio clock,
the birds' courting in June's first light, beside me
your body hot and naked, your face moored
in night's pocket. Out the window Eos lays her pink razzle
across pillows of cloud, a woodpecker's tock-tock-tock at
the electric pole down by the road, jays hector and squabble
over the fern field, the thrush's near piccolo rings over the roof.
It's the same razzmatazz every morning, and you, your face still
in the pillow, a pocket's warm secret.
                              Sunrise. Light spokes out
from the pink heel of hand set on the horizon in the pines, Liberty's
crown signing in. New York's fine again, Whitman's transfigured
humanity's crossing Time, ferrying us back and forth
as he said would continue. Achilles' bronze shield propped
on the disarrayed floor of the tent, lit and polished
for a respite from war, and saintly Earth leans on her tilted
spine toward the sun. Hum of hummingbirds content on the porch
at the hanging fuchsias, blood-red throat of the thrush—our jumble
of hips starts in the blue sheets, Caravaggio's swing-hipped
sensual angels—What music!—and the radio
bursts—Jimi Hendrix straight as a heron in cool water,
the aching strings shot with vermillion flowers.

Anne Harding Woodworth

## First Kiss, 1957

*a glosa*

> i don't recall what happened next.
> i kept you at a distance.
> but tangled in a knot of sex
> my punishment was lifted.
>       Leonard Cohen, from "Drank a Lot," in
>       *The Flame* (2018, Picador), p. 73

A teen I was, those walk-away years,
a teen with curly hair
and ignorance of love and lust
and you, a running mystery.
I studied you, I shied from you.
I sometimes felt perplexed
at what strange things you talked about.
I watched you in your games,
and then you kissed me. I was vexed!
I don't recall what happened next.

Well, yes, I do remember vaguely
feeling shame and guilt.
I wondered what had happened to me.
Would I figure out
the meaning of a stolen kiss—
me, showing no resistance?
I couldn't ask my mother, no,
she'd lecture me on morals
and words of teenage abstinence
to keep you at a distance.

*Woodworth*

And yet, I couldn't stay away
from kisses and where they led.
I found myself in places where
I truly liked to be.
You lured me into ecstasy,
no balances or checks.
I did some things I shouldn't have.
I knew I liked what you could do.
I knew those causes and effects
got tangled in a knot of sex.

I'd been doing what I oughtn't.
My guilt became a force,
when all at once I strung some words
together in a verse.
Writing down in rhyming words—
how my heart felt gifted.
Poems filled my life with you.
You came to be my muse.
I knew my focus bravely shifted.
My punishment was lifted.

## Certificates in Safe Deposit

When Lincoln died, Mary gave his favorite cane
to Frederick Douglass—who called it, and I quote, a staff.
I've seen a photograph of his thank-you note.

That kind of proof is what I need, as in the bank,
the keeper's key will join with mine to open up
the door and drawer of proof that I was born.
I'm not aloof from this—

it's certified on parchment edged in gold.
I even have a name, a county for my birth,
which means, I guess, I hold a place on earth.

It gives me, too, a mother and a sire.
Ah, here I find certificates entire, that show
I was a wife in early life. Two others prove
my marriage ended before another made its move.

But what is this? I see the word *deceased*, its date,
its place, its hour in black and inky scrawl. Is there
any other way to learn I do or don't still walk alert,
or if I ever breathed at all? Come walk with me

and Mr. Douglass now. He holds the Lincoln cane in hand,
on both sides of the river day and night, a handsome man,
hair a halo bright. And after we have walked,

I'll leave to you a gift of words that also prove I lived,
Words that have supported me. I wrote and felt secure.
No need for a thank-you note.

## Train Station

> *To be a train station of existence is no small matter.*
> Jane Hirshfield, from her poem "Tin"

I am the Summit Train Station of the 1950s,
where the word Lackawanna was woven
into my cloth, back when I played jacks
and jumped rope. All in together, girls.

I'm the train station that contained evenings
when we picked up my father arriving on the 6:45
from Hoboken, my mother waiting in the car
in a cobblestone-sloped parking lot.

We kids played on the platform under
the tin roof of a canopy, a slalom between columns,
always protected from the snow or rain.
How do you like the weather, girls?

The train arrived, heavy and loud. I felt alone
as it approached, spitting steam at me, as dads
stepped down, going to those waiting, or alone
to their car parked since early morning.

My days are long, my siding crumbling.
I contain in me the waiting, timetables, tickets,
conducting. I am still the Summit station,
though I've changed names and switched tracks.

The world moves slowly toward me, then away from me,
gains speed, anticipates curves. I take my bag with me,
sit with it on my lap. I guard what's in it, a line, a verse,
next to the lady with the alligator purse.

## Late Summer into Winter

*a glosa*

> *Leaves, you may linger in the fall sunset*
> *Like late lingering butterflies before frost.*
> *Treetops, you may sift the sunset cross-lights*
> *Spreading a loose checkerwork of gold and shadow.*
>     Carl Sandburg, from "Haze Gold," in
>     *Good Morning America* (Crosby Gaige,
>     1928), p. 73

You, willows, need no permit to weep
nor you, bleeding hearts, to arch your stems.
What's going to happen in nature will—
just look at you, reeds, edging the rill.
And you, sycamores, who follow the code
from seed to grown, no law unmet,
as bark peels off from your sturdy bole,
while you, sweet maples, prepare for the cold,
chestnuts fearing the castanet.
Leaves, you may linger in the fall sunset.

Monarch, you've left the chrysalis blank,
envisioning south as the place to go.
But first on nectars you feed and flap,
as breezes of autumn begin to blow,
and xylem, phloem slow their sap.
Fall is coming, summer's lost.
Leaves, you're collecting in woods and towns,
oranges, yellows, reds and browns.
You cling to branches at all cost
like butterflies lingering before the frost.

The days are shortening—they follow the code.
Morning gets darker and waking is hard.
The kids pack their lunches in darkness of day.
The lamps of their home burn early to start.
They walk to their school as if it were night,
and yellow buses turn on their lights.
When Saturday comes the kids have all day
to run in the sun, to play in the rays
that stay on only 'til four o'clock strikes.
And you, treetops, sift the sunset cross-lights.

When autumn has come and winter is here,
the bears in the woods eat to sustain
life in their cave through the end of the year.
The blue jays don't mind the cold winter air.
nor do the squirrels outside the wolf's lair.
And so the sun shines on the young and the old.
Of course, we think that we can endure
the natural code of behavior,
as long as we're warm and the sun remains gold
and spreads checkered shadows amid the cold.

## Scripts

*of the unsung*

Think of the words written
and never read or spoken
on stage or in film.

Think of the curtain calls not taken,
the lyrics never sung,
poems not published.

Reams of paper turn brittle
and yellow in a file drawer,
dry out through no fault of their own

like hair that grays and thins,
and joints that hurt more each day.
And so the cast of characters

grows old, their banter
never heard, lying still in runes
that sing only on the page.

Exit, exeunt.
One does, they do,
without ever having entered.

# Bios & Acknowledgments

Many thanks to the editors who first published some of the poems in this book.

## Patricia Gray

Patricia Gray was born in Washington, D.C. but grew up, after the age of five, in Virginia's Shenandoah Valley. After receiving an MFA, she accepted a position at the Library of Congress, where she created the popular Poetry at Noon program. A selected participant at Bread Loaf Writer's Conference in 2004 and 2006, she was a presenting author at South Carolina Book Festival in 2006. In 2023, her hybrid poem, "Morning of Wilderness and Wind" was a finalist for the 55th Millennium Writing Award. Also that year, Patricia won her seventh Artist Fellowship in Poetry from the DC Commission on the Arts and Humanities. In 2025, her poems appeared in *The Ravens Perch, Ground Journal, The Plentitudes, The Mid-Atlantic Review* and *Hill Rag*. She teaches creative writing for The Writer's Center in Bethesda, Maryland and enjoys the heck out of Zoom meetings with writers in the U.S. and abroad.

The following poems, or versions thereof, appeared in these publications:
"July Full Moon" in *Stickman Review*, Winter 2015
"Falling" on *the poet's billow* website, as a semi-finalist for The Atlantis Award, 2022
"Crossing the Blue Ridge" in *The Mid-Atlantic Review*, February 25, 2025.
"My Uncle's House" in *Rupture: poems* by Patricia Gray from Red Hen Press, 2005
"Washington Days" in *forpoetry.com* in 2005 and in *Beltway Poetry Quarterly*'s DC Places issue, Summer 2006.

## Charise M. Hoge

Charise M. Hoge, MA, MSW, is a writer, dance/movement therapist, and performing artist. Her work in the healing arts includes programs for hospitals, counseling centers, businesses, the National Zoo, United States Holocaust Memorial Museum, and the World Bank. She is co-author of *Meet Your Muse:*

*The Dance of Creativity* and *A Portable Identity: Your Guide to Taking Charge of Change Abroad*, and author of three poetry collections: *Striking Light from Ashes*, *Muse in a Suitcase*, and *Inheritance of Flowers*. Her poetry is also featured in the book *Next Line, Please: Prompts to Inspire Poets and Writers* (edited by David Lehman). She has been a guest author for *The Best American Poetry blog* and featured poet for *The WildStory Podcast*. Based in the Washington, DC area, Charise and her husband regularly escape to West Virginia where she is poet-in-residence for *Art on Cullers Run*, Mathias. www.charisehoge.com

"Flow" is included in the collection *Muse in a Suitcase*, published by Kelsay Books, 2021.
"Wild Goose Chase" first appeared in *The Examined Life: The Literary Journal of the University of Iowa Carver College of Medicine*, Vol.10, 2023, p.137.

## Mary Ann Larkin

Mary Ann Larkin is the author of a full-length book, *That Deep and Steady Hum*, and six chapbooks of poetry. Her work has appeared in *Poetry Greece, Poetry Ireland Review, New Letters, The Greensboro Review* and other journals and in more than twenty anthologies, including Harry N. Abrams' series on poetry and art. She was a co-founder of The Big Mama Poetry Troupe, a group of five feminist poets based in Cleveland in the seventies, who performed from Chicago to New York City. Larkin has taught writing at a number of colleges, most recently at Howard University, and written for NPR, NIH, Foundation News and others. She has enjoyed residencies at both Yaddo and the Jentel Foundation in Wyoming. She co-founded Pond Road Press, which published *Tough Heaven: Poems of Pittsburgh* by Jack Gilbert. Born in Pittsburgh, Pennsylvania, she lives with her husband Patric Pepper on Cape Cod in North Truro, Massachusetts.

*That Deep and Steady Hum,* Broadkill River Press, Milton, Delaware, 2010: "Angell's Toenails" and "Those Desert Afternoons"
*The Greensboro Review:* "It"
*On Gannon Street,* Broadkill River Press, Milton, Delaware, 2015 "The Grandmothers," also published in *Josephine Quarterly* and *Off the Coast*.
*Humana Obscura:* "A Lock of Patric's Mother's Hair"

## Greg McBride

Greg McBride is the author of *Guest of Time* (Pond Road Press, 2023), *Porthole* (Briery Creek Press, 2012), and *Back of the Envelope* (Southeast Missouri State University Press, 2009). His work appears in *Alaska Quarterly, Bellevue, The Best American Poetry, Boulevard, Gettysburg Review, Rhino, River Styx, Salmagundi, Southern Poetry Review*, and elsewhere. His awards include the Liam Rector First Book Prize for Poetry for *Porthole*, the *Boulevard* Emerging Poet prize, and grants in poetry from the Maryland State Arts Council. A Vietnam veteran and lawyer, he is the founding editor of the *Innisfree Poetry Journal*.

*Valparaiso Poetry Review:* "Crossing Over," "Whistled Alive"
*Connecticut Review:* "In Country: Day One"
*Salmagundi:* "Music Lady"
*The Best American Poetry* and *Fotospecchio:* "Know Thyself"
*Bellevue Literary Review:* "Back of the Envelope"
*Legal Studies Forum:* "The Buffalo"

## Nancy Fitz-Hugh Meneely

After retiring from FEMA, Nancy Fitz-Hugh Meneely moved from D.C. to Connecticut to pursue what Baron Wormser calls "the poetry life". She thrives by her association with several shoreline poetry groups and her renewed membership in the Capitol Hill Poetry Group. With Gray Jacobik, she founded an ongoing week-long poetry retreat for Frost Place Alums. Her first book, *Letter from Italy, 1944* (Antrim House) was noted by the *Hartford Courant* as one of thirteen important books published in 2013 by Connecticut writers. It provided the libretto for an oratorio performed in 2013 by the GM Chorale with the Yale Symphony Orchestra and in 2017 by the Hartford Chorale with the Hartford Symphony Orchestra. Her second book, *Simple Absence* (Antrim House), was nominated for The National Book Award and placed as a Grand Prize Finalist for the 2021 Next Generation Indie Awards and the 2021 Eric Hoffer Award.

## Jean Nordhaus

Jean Nordhaus's eight volumes of poetry include *A Bracelet of Lies* (Washington Writers' Publishing House), *The Porcelain Apes of Moses Mendelssohn* (Milkweed Editions), *Innocence* (Ohio State University Press), *Memos from the Broken World* (Mayapple Press), *My Life in Hiding* (Quarterly Review of Literature), and, most recently, *The Music of Being* (Broadstone Books) plus two chapbooks. Her work has appeared in *American Poetry Review*, *The New Republic*, *Poetry,* and numerous other venues. Over 60 of her reviews, articles, and essays on dance and poetry have been published in *The Washington Post*, *The Washington Review*, and other publications. She formerly served as poetry coordinator at the Folger Shakespeare Library, President of Washington Writers' Publishing House, and, for eight years, as Review Editor of *Poet Lore*. She lives on Capitol Hill in Washington, DC and part-time in Taos, New Mexico.

"Gloves" appeared originally in *Window*, and subsequently in *A Language of Hands* (SCOP, 1982)
"The Aunts" appeared originally in *The Centennial Review* and subsequently in *A Bracelet of Lies* (WWPH, 1987)
"The Stammer" appeared originally in *Poetry* and subsequently in the chapbook *A Purchase of Porcelain* (The Kinloch Rivers Chapbook Competition, 1998) and *The Porcelain Apes of Moses Mendelssohn* (Milkweed Editions, 2002)
"The Innocent" appeared originally in *West Branch* and subsequently in *Innocence* (Ohio State University Press, 2006)
"I Was Always Leaving" appeared originally in *Gettysburg Review* and subsequently in *Memos from the Broken World* (Mayapple Press, 2016)
"Selling the Porsche" appeared originally in *Sow's Ear Poetry Review* and subsequently in *The Music of Being* (Broadstone Books, 2023)
"Old Money" appears in *Innisfree* #40

## Patric Pepper

Patric Pepper holds a Bachelor of Arts in Philosophy from the University of Maryland and is a retired process engineer. He has published three poetry chapbooks, including *Everything Pure as Nothing,* from Finishing Line Press, and a full length collection, *Temporary Apprehensions,* winner of the

Washington Writers' Publishing House (WWPH) Poetry Prize. He has volunteered in various roles with small press publishers and organizations since the mid 1970s as a reviewer, reader, book designer, facilities manager, board member, various clerical roles, and president for six years of a 501(c)3 cooperative publishing house, WWPH. Patric is a founding editor of a poetry micro-press, Pond Road Press, which has published 15 books and chapbooks to date, including Jack Gilbert's *Tough Heaven: Poems of Pittsburgh*. His poetry and reviews have appeared in various journals and magazines since 1974, most recently in the WWPH anthology *America's Future, Backbone Mountain Review, The Mid-Atlantic Review, Full Bleed,* and *The Innisfree Poetry Journal*. Pepper lives on Cape Cod with his wife, Mary Ann Larkin.

*Full Bleed:* "The Old Homeplace Is Inside You"
*Innisfree Poetry Journal:* "Number 6 Sherman Circle"
*The Northern Virginia Review:* "Swept"
*Okay Donkey Magazine:* "They're Grackles and Every Time I See Them"

## Noel Salinger

Noel joined the Capitol Hill Poetry Group recently. He retired in 2018 after a 40-year career in non-profit development, mostly at the American Civil Liberties Union, the University of Chicago, and the Smithsonian. Since retirement from decades of professional writing, Noel has returned to poetry, which he has been writing since his teens. Noel attended Syracuse University, where he studied poetry writing with Stephen Dunn and Philip Booth, and earned a master's degree in anthropology from the University of Chicago. He lives with his wife LeAnne Sawyers, a painter, and her mother in North Potomac, Maryland.

"Pioneers" was previously published by the journal *Passager*, receiving an honorable mention in its Fall 2024 poetry contest.

## Rosemary Winslow

When four, sitting on the floor listening to my father read from the King James Bible, I became aware that the sounds were waves in the air. I was in awe at the beauty and fell in love right there with the sounds of poetry and music. I wrote poems in loops of e's before I knew how to read. First poem:

age seven. I've published two books of poems, co-edited a book of essays on beauty, written dozens of researched articles on poetry, rhetoric, and writing, including entries on prosody, meter, versification, pitch, and others in *The Princeton Encyclopedia of Poetry and Poetics, Fourth Edition*, *The Walt Whitman Encyclopedia*, *Encyclopedia of Twentieth-Century American Poetry*, and numerous journals. She and her husband, John Winslow, host poetry readings—Sounds on M Street—in his painting studio. She taught literature and writing for 50 years. She is retired from the faculty of the Catholic University of America.

"Going Home" first appeared in *The Southern Review*, reprinted in *The Breath of Parted Lips": Voices from the Robert Frost Place Volume II*, edited by Sydney Lea, Cavan Kerry Press.
"Foxes" first appeared in *Beltway Poetry Journal*, reprinted in *Green Bodies*, The Word Works.
"Kingdom of Cloth, Three Women, A Naked Boy" first appeared in *Valparaiso Poetry Review*, reprinted in *Green Bodies*.
"Haifa Street" first appeared in *Locus Point II*, reprinted in *Defying Gravity*, David Robert Books.
"This Quiet Time" first appeared in *Gargoyle*.
"Blue Raft" first appeared in *The Cafe Review*, reprinted in *Defying Gravity*.

## Anne Harding Woodworth

Anne Harding Woodworth, poet and playwright, is the author of nine books of poetry and five chapbooks. Her book, *Trouble*, received the 2022 William Meredith Poetry Award. Her chapbook, *The Last Gun*, won the COG Poetry Award, and an excerpt of it was subsequently animated (see https://vimeo/193842252). Anne's most recent book of poetry is *Merely Players*, which focuses on performance—including theatre, cinema, dance, magic, mime, music, puppetry, even the soccer field. Anne reads her poetry frequently, virtually and in person. She is currently at work on two plays with her sister, playwright Bundy H. Boit. When Anne is not in Washington, D.C., she can be found at her cabin in the mountains of Western North Carolina.

"Scripts," appears in her book *Merely Players* (2025, Turning Point).

www.ingramcontent.com/pod-product-compliance
Lightning Source LLC
Chambersburg PA
CBHW030908170426
43193CB00009BA/776